TORONTO BLUE JAYS BOOK

FOR KIDS

The Young Fan's Guide To Baseball Dreams

Nora H. Jose

Toronto Blue Jays Book For Kids

TABLE OF CONTENTS

INTRODUCTION

Welcome to the exciting world of the **Toronto Blue Jays**, where baseball magic fills the air and dreams take flight high above the diamond! This book is made especially for young fans who love cheering, learning, and imagining what it feels like to stand beneath the bright lights of the big stadium. Every story in these pages celebrates the joy of the game, the teamwork that makes champions, and the spirit that keeps players believing in themselves no matter what challenges they face.

In the heart of **Toronto**, a city full of color, sound, and energy, the Blue Jays bring people together through the power of sport. Families, friends, and fans fill the stands, waving flags, clapping hands, and singing songs that echo through the sky. The sound of a bat cracking, a ball soaring, and a crowd roaring creates moments that stay in hearts forever. Baseball becomes more than just a game—it turns into a memory shared across generations.

From their very first swing in 1977, the Blue Jays showed the world that determination, passion, and practice can turn small beginnings into great success. Their journey reminds young readers that even dreams born in one city can reach across countries and inspire people everywhere. With effort and courage, the impossible becomes possible, and the smallest hopeful wish can lead to the biggest victory.

Each player who wears the Blue Jays uniform carries a story of growth, challenge, and discovery. Some grew up tossing baseballs in quiet parks, others learned from family and friends, but all shared one goal—to give their best and never give up. Together, they create a family built on friendship, hard work, and belief in one another. Through every inning, they prove that teamwork shines brighter than any spotlight.

The Blue Jays' history is filled with thrilling plays, unforgettable home runs, and moments that changed baseball forever. From World Series triumphs to comeback wins, the team's journey continues to inspire kids everywhere to chase their own goals with confidence and joy. Every swing teaches a lesson about courage, every catch shows the value of focus, and every cheer reminds us that support makes success even sweeter.

As you open these pages, imagine yourself stepping onto the field, feeling the grass beneath your shoes, and looking up at the endless sky above the Rogers Centre. Let the Blue Jays guide your imagination, fuel your determination, and show that dreams really can come true. Whether you're holding a glove, a bat, or just a big dream in your heart, this adventure is for you—because every great story starts with belief, and yours begins right here.

CHAPTER 1: THE BEGINNING OF A DREAM

Long before the roar of the crowd filled the air, the dream of a baseball team in Toronto was just a quiet wish carried by hopeful hearts. People imagined players in bright uniforms, running across green fields, swinging bats beneath shining lights. Every idea, every plan, and every meeting started with one simple thought—*what if Toronto had its own team to cheer for?* From that spark, something incredible began to grow.

In those early days, excitement buzzed through the city like never before. Kids tossed balls on sidewalks, pretending to be stars they had only seen on television. Parents talked about games that could unite the community and bring joy to families all year long. It wasn't only about sport—it was about pride, belonging, and a shared vision for something special.

The people who worked to create the team faced big challenges, but their belief never faded. They searched for the perfect name, colors, and symbol to represent Canada's largest city. The idea of a blue jay—strong, swift, and full of spirit—fit perfectly. The Blue Jays were born from courage, creativity, and love for the game.

When the team finally took shape, it brought hope to every corner of Toronto. Schools, parks, and playgrounds buzzed with talk of baseball. Children started collecting caps, jerseys, and posters, dreaming of someday playing under the same sky. Those dreams became the heart of the Blue Jays story.

The creation of the team wasn't just about players or fields; it was about building something that could unite people. Baseball became a bridge between generations, connecting young and old through laughter, teamwork, and pride. Each swing of the bat told a story of determination, each cheer carried the rhythm of possibility.

That beginning marked more than the start of a franchise—it marked the birth of a community. From one dream came thousands more, all shining together like stars above the diamond. Every fan, from the youngest to the oldest, became part of something greater: a story that would inspire forever.

1.1 The Birth of a Team

When the Toronto Blue Jays officially joined Major League Baseball in 1977, history took a new turn. The announcement filled hearts with joy, and children across the country began to imagine themselves as future players wearing the team's bright blue. It was a moment when hope turned into reality, and the city finally had a team to call its own.

Building the team was no small task. Coaches, scouts, and leaders searched far and wide for talent—athletes with passion, energy, and the will to win. Each player chosen carried a dream of representing not just a team, but a whole nation. The excitement of something brand-new filled the air.

Opening day arrived with thunderous applause. Fans packed the stands, waving banners, clapping hands, and shouting cheers that echoed through the stadium. Even though rain fell from the clouds, spirits remained bright. The Blue Jays took the field, ready to write their first chapter in baseball history.

Every pitch, every catch, and every swing mattered that day. The scoreboard didn't just measure runs—it measured belief. Though victories were still to come, the energy of that moment proved that the Blue Jays belonged. The players' determination painted the city in shades of blue and white.

From that day forward, the team became part of Toronto's heartbeat. Games brought neighbors together, and children filled backyards with laughter as they practiced their favorite plays. The dream that began quietly now echoed through homes, schools, and hearts across Canada.

The birth of the team gave young fans a reason to dream big. It showed that when people unite behind an idea, amazing things can happen. The Blue Jays became a symbol of courage, teamwork, and endless possibilities—a shining reminder that every beginning holds the power to change everything.

1.2 A City Ready for Baseball

Toronto had long waited for the crack of a bat and the cheers of a baseball crowd. Before the Blue Jays arrived, sports fans dreamed of sunny afternoons filled with home runs, daring steals, and thrilling plays. The city, already full of life, needed something new—something that would bring everyone together through joy and excitement.

When the team was announced, the entire community came alive. Posters appeared in shop windows, newspapers filled with stories, and schools buzzed with talk of players soon to wear the maple leaf proudly. It wasn't just about games; it was about spirit, pride, and connection.

Families began planning their trips to the stadium, eager to see their heroes in action. For many, it was their first time watching professional baseball live. Parents explained the rules to curious children, who listened with wide eyes and endless wonder. The game became more than a pastime—it became a family tradition.

Toronto's skyline, already grand, found new color with the Blue Jays' arrival. The stadium lights joined the city glow, shining hope across neighborhoods and parks. Every street corner seemed to hum with anticipation, as if the whole place was preparing for something extraordinary.

Businesses, schools, and communities joined in the celebration. People wore team caps, displayed blue flags, and even painted murals to welcome their new heroes. The Blue Jays weren't just a team—they were a movement that brought unity, laughter, and pride.

The city had been ready for baseball for years, and when the first pitch was thrown, it was as if Toronto finally took a deep, joyful breath. From that day on, every fan knew the truth: baseball had found its perfect home in Canada's largest city.

1.3 The First Swing of Hope

The first time a Blue Jays player stepped up to the plate, hearts pounded across the stadium. Children leaned forward in their seats, hands gripping souvenirs, eyes locked on the batter. The sound of the bat meeting the ball echoed like a promise—hope had arrived, and it wore blue.

That swing symbolized more than a start; it represented years of waiting, working, and wishing. The crowd's roar carried far beyond the field, through streets and homes, into every young dreamer's imagination. In that moment, Toronto believed that anything was possible.

Players gave their all, not just to win games but to prove that dedication could build greatness. Each movement, each run, each catch told a story of teamwork and faith. Even the smallest play felt meaningful, filled with purpose and excitement.

For young fans, that first swing became a symbol of possibility. Kids grabbed bats, practiced in parks, and shouted, "Go Jays!" with all their hearts. The dream wasn't just for professionals anymore—it belonged to every child who dared to believe.

The feeling spread quickly, lighting up hearts across Canada. Baseball diamonds filled with laughter, practice sessions, and friendly games. Coaches encouraged their players to work hard, reminding them that big things start with small steps.

The first swing didn't just mark a new beginning—it planted seeds of inspiration that would grow for generations. From that moment forward, the Toronto Blue Jays became more than a team—they became a symbol of hope, heart, and the power of believing in dreams.

1.4 Fans Who Believed from the Start

Before the wins, before the trophies, there were fans who believed with every heartbeat. They stood by the team through rain, losses, and challenges, always cheering, always hoping. Their voices built the foundation of something lasting—a family that would grow stronger with every season.

Children painted their faces blue and white, waving banners proudly in the stands. Parents clapped, sang, and taught their little ones to love the game. Every fan, no matter their age, felt part of something bigger than themselves. Together, they made the stadium come alive.

Even when the team struggled in early years, the fans never gave up. Their cheers carried the players forward, turning setbacks into lessons. That unshakable support showed the world that true loyalty shines brightest during difficult times.

Some fans traveled long distances just to see their heroes play. Others listened to games on the radio or watched on television, celebrating every hit, catch, and home run as if they were there in person. The connection between the team and its followers grew stronger every day.

Through laughter, songs, and countless memories, the Blue Jays' community became a source of pride for Toronto and the entire country. The energy inside the stadium felt like magic—hopeful, bright, and full of love for the game.

The fans who believed from the beginning helped shape the Blue Jays' story. Their faith turned a new team into a symbol of unity, courage, and joy. To this day, their spirit lives on in every cheer, reminding everyone that dreams come true when hearts stay faithful.

CHAPTER 2: THE BLUE AND WHITE SPIRIT

From the moment the Toronto Blue Jays took the field, their colors—bright blue and crisp white—became a symbol of pride, strength, and unity. Those colors waved on flags, shone on jerseys, and sparkled in the eyes of fans everywhere. Each hue carried meaning: blue for courage and confidence, white for honesty and hope. Together, they told the story of a team built on dreams and determination.

In every corner of Toronto, the spirit of the Blue Jays began to bloom. Children wore caps with the team's logo, proud to show their support. Schools held baseball days, and parks filled with young players swinging bats and chasing fly balls. The energy spread far beyond the stadium, connecting families through laughter and love for the game.

The Blue Jays' spirit was more than color and design—it was an attitude. It taught people to face challenges bravely, play fairly, and cheer loudly. Whether the team won or lost, fans stood tall, knowing that true sportsmanship means giving your best at all times. The Blue and White Spirit became a way of life for everyone who believed in the team.

Players carried that energy with them wherever they traveled. On the road, in different cities, they represented not just Toronto but the entire nation of Canada. Their uniforms weren't just clothing—they were symbols of pride that reminded everyone of home.

As time passed, the spirit grew even stronger. It united people from different places, languages, and backgrounds under one banner. Baseball became a bridge of friendship, and the Blue Jays' message of togetherness reached hearts far and wide.

Every time the team stepped onto the diamond, the spirit shone bright. The blue skies above seemed to mirror their colors, and the cheers from fans echoed like music through the air. That energy—powerful, joyful, and unstoppable—made every game feel like something special.

2.1 Building Team Colors and Pride

Choosing the perfect colors for the Blue Jays wasn't just about fashion—it was about meaning. Designers wanted something that reflected Canada's heart while standing out on the baseball field. The choice of blue and white felt right from the start, symbolizing loyalty, peace, and bold ambition.

The blue reminded fans of open skies, freedom, and endless possibilities. The white reflected purity, unity, and fairness. When stitched together on a jersey, those shades became more than fabric—they became identity.

Every player who put on that uniform carried a promise to play with integrity and pride.

The city embraced the look immediately. Shop windows displayed new merchandise, and children saved their allowance to buy caps and shirts. Wearing Blue Jays colors became a statement of belonging, a way to say, "I believe in this team."

Artists painted murals of soaring blue jays across walls and bridges. Schools decorated classrooms with banners and posters. Even buses displayed team slogans, turning the streets into rivers of blue and white. Everywhere you looked, the city glowed with excitement.

As the team grew stronger, so did the pride behind the colors. Victories made the shades brighter, while tough seasons made them deeper, richer, and even more meaningful. The colors became a part of Toronto's story—symbols of hope that continued to shine through every challenge.

Each time fans wear those hues, they celebrate more than baseball—they celebrate courage, unity, and the spirit of believing in something bigger than themselves. The Blue Jays' colors remind everyone that dreams painted with heart can never fade.

2.2 The Power of the Blue Jay Bird

The Blue Jay bird isn't just beautiful—it's brave. Known for its intelligence and fearlessness, this bright-feathered creature became the perfect symbol for Toronto's baseball team. It represents confidence, loyalty, and teamwork—qualities every great player and fan should have.

Blue Jays are small but mighty, unafraid to protect their nests or face bigger birds. That same spirit lives inside every player who wears the team logo. Whether facing strong opponents or tough challenges, the team always plays with courage and determination.

The bird's bold color inspired fans to stand out too. Its blue feathers shimmer under sunlight, just like the team's uniforms under stadium lights. The Blue Jay's clear, cheerful call reminds everyone to speak up, stay positive, and never back down.

Children quickly fell in love with the mascot, seeing it as both a friend and a hero. They learned that being a Blue Jay meant showing kindness while staying strong. It wasn't about size or power—it was about heart.

Nature and baseball blended beautifully in this symbol. Every time a Blue Jay bird flew over Toronto, people smiled, thinking of their favorite team. It was as if the city and its spirit were connected by wings of hope.

The power of the Blue Jay bird goes far beyond feathers and flight—it lives in the hearts of fans and players alike. Its courage reminds everyone to rise, dream, and soar higher every day.

2.3 Songs, Cheers, and Stadium Smiles

When game day arrives, the Rogers Centre fills with the happiest sounds you can imagine. Fans clap, stomp, and sing together, turning the stadium into a sea of joy. The Blue Jays' songs echo through the air, lifting spirits and creating memories that last a lifetime.

From the first pitch to the final out, every cheer matters. Kids wave flags, parents take pictures, and friends share snacks while laughing and shouting for their favorite players. The rhythm of the crowd feels like music—a heartbeat that keeps the game alive.

Special chants and melodies fill the air whenever the team takes the field. "Let's go, Blue Jays!" rings out loud and clear, bouncing off every seat and roof. Even when the score is close, fans never stop believing. Their voices push the players forward with courage and pride.

Smiles are everywhere—on faces painted blue, on people dancing in the aisles, on mascots waving high-fives. Every laugh adds to the magic. Baseball, for the Blue Jays community, is not just a sport—it's a celebration of togetherness.

Children learn the cheers quickly, joining in with excitement. Singing those songs makes them feel part of something big, something wonderful. It's a reminder that even one voice can make a difference when joined with others in joy.

As the game ends and fans head home, the songs still echo in their hearts. The music of baseball, the laughter of friends, and the cheers of thousands blend into a memory that shines long after the lights go out.

2.4 The Magic of Rogers Centre

Rising proudly beside the CN Tower, the **Rogers Centre** is more than a ballpark—it's a home filled with stories, laughter, and dreams. Its giant roof opens to the sky, letting sunlight pour over the field while the city skyline sparkles nearby. For fans, walking inside feels like stepping into a world of wonder.

Every seat offers a view of something special: the green grass, the white lines, and the Blue Jays logo shining at the center. When the team runs out, cheers thunder like waves. The sound fills every corner, making hearts race and smiles grow wide.

Kids love watching the roof glide open, revealing clouds and stars above the game. It feels like the whole universe is watching, cheering along with them. The stadium becomes a magical place where dreams come alive under the open sky.

Concession stands serve delicious treats, and the smell of popcorn and hotdogs fills the air. Families laugh, wave foam fingers, and take photos to remember every special moment. Every inning brings new surprises and excitement.

The Rogers Centre isn't just a building—it's a gathering place for love, friendship, and joy. It brings together people from all over Canada and beyond to celebrate the beautiful game of baseball.

As night falls and lights twinkle across Toronto, the stadium glows like a beacon of happiness. Inside its walls, the spirit of the Blue Jays continues to shine bright—reminding every young fan that magic happens when dreams take flight.

CHAPTER 3: HEROES ON THE FIELD

Every team has players who shine brightly, but the Toronto Blue Jays have heroes who light up hearts as much as they light up the scoreboard. These athletes are more than just names on jerseys—they are dreamers, leaders, and role models who inspire every young fan watching from the stands. Their courage, skill, and love for the game remind everyone that greatness begins with believing in yourself.

When the Blue Jays take the field, they carry the hopes of an entire nation. Each player steps up with confidence, ready to give their best for their teammates and their fans. The sound of a bat meeting the ball, the leap of an outfielder catching a fly, the cheer of the crowd—these moments create magic that lives forever.

The heroes of the Blue Jays didn't all start as stars. Many began as children in parks, practicing throws, dreaming of one day playing under the bright lights. Their journeys were filled with challenges, hard work, and determination. But through every struggle, they kept believing that their time would come.

Fans admire their bravery and heart. They see how players handle both victory and defeat—with grace, respect, and humility. Every athlete teaches that being a hero isn't about perfection; it's about effort, teamwork, and never giving up.

The players' dedication shines both on and off the field. They visit schools, support charities, and encourage kids to dream big. Their kindness off the diamond is just as powerful as their talent during the game.

These Blue Jays heroes remind every young reader that real strength comes from character. Their story is proof that heroes aren't born—they're made through patience, practice, and a heart full of passion.

3.1 Meet the First Blue Jays

The very first Blue Jays team in 1977 was a group of dreamers ready to make history. They came from different places, but all shared the same love for baseball. Each player carried excitement, nerves, and pride as they stepped onto the field wearing Toronto's colors for the first time.

Those early days were filled with learning and growing together. The team didn't win every game, but they played with heart, courage, and determination. Fans saw how much effort they gave, and that inspired loyalty that still lasts today. Every swing and every pitch carried hope for the future.

Players like **Doug Ault**, who hit the team's first home run, became instant legends. His powerful swing and big smile brought joy to thousands. Teammates worked hard, practiced daily, and trusted each other through ups and downs.

The coaches guided the young team with patience, teaching them teamwork, timing, and belief. The bond between players grew stronger with every inning. They weren't just a baseball club—they were a family learning to fly together.

Toronto fans fell in love quickly. The crowd's cheers echoed through the city, lifting spirits even during tough losses. The connection between the city and the team deepened as people saw how hard those players tried.

The first Blue Jays laid the foundation for greatness. Their courage and commitment built a tradition of strength that continues to inspire new generations of fans and players alike.

3.2 Star Players Who Made History

Throughout the years, the Blue Jays have been home to incredible stars who changed baseball forever. These players became legends through their amazing skills, determination, and leadership. Each one left a mark on the team's story that will never fade.

Roberto Alomar, with his quick reflexes and golden glove, brought energy and brilliance to every game. His smooth defense and fearless attitude helped lead the Blue Jays to glory. Young fans loved how he played with both talent and joy.

Joe Carter became a hero with one unforgettable swing—the home run that won the 1993 World Series. His jump of excitement after that hit became a moment frozen in time. Every fan watching that day felt the pride of Canada shining bright.

Roy Halladay, known for his hard work and quiet strength, inspired teammates through dedication. His powerful pitching and steady focus showed kids that greatness comes from preparation, not luck. His legacy continues to motivate players everywhere.

Then came **Vladimir Guerrero Jr.**, a new generation star carrying his father's passion and his own fire. His big smile, strong swing, and love for the fans made him a favorite around the world. He represents the future of the Blue Jays' dream.

Each of these athletes showed that success comes from heart, effort, and belief. Their stories remind every reader that heroes are made by what they give, not just what they achieve.

3.3 Coaches Who Taught Greatness

Behind every great player stands a coach who believes in them. For the Blue Jays, coaches have always been guides, teachers, and mentors. They shape not just the team's performance, but the players' character, helping each one find confidence and purpose.

In the beginning, coaches worked tirelessly to build discipline and unity. They taught fundamentals—how to field, hit, throw, and most importantly, how to trust each other. They knew that teamwork wins more games than talent alone.

Coaches like **Cito Gaston** made history as the first Black manager to win a World Series. His leadership brought calm, wisdom, and encouragement. Players respected him deeply for his fairness, focus, and belief in every member of the team.

Through wins and losses, coaches stayed steady, reminding players to keep learning. They turned mistakes into lessons and pressure into opportunity. Their words gave players strength when times were tough and confidence when spirits were low.

Many young fans don't see all the work coaches do behind the scenes—planning strategies, giving advice, and building trust. Yet without them, the team's success would never shine as brightly.

The Blue Jays' coaches have always been teachers of both baseball and life. Their patience, passion, and leadership have helped turn good players into legends, and dreamers into believers.

3.4 Legends That Inspire Young Fans

Legends of the Blue Jays live in every story told at schoolyards, living rooms, and baseball fields across Canada. Their achievements echo through time, inspiring new fans to pick up bats, wear jerseys, and dream of hitting the winning run.

Kids look up to players like **José Bautista**, whose powerful bat and fiery spirit made crowds cheer wildly. His famous "bat flip" wasn't just a celebration—it was a symbol of confidence, joy, and believing in yourself.

Others admire **Carlos Delgado**, a player who gave back to his community and led with kindness. He reminded everyone that heroes care about people, not just trophies. His generosity and love for fans made him unforgettable.

Legends also teach valuable lessons about resilience. They faced injuries, tough seasons, and pressure, yet never stopped striving for excellence. Their stories show that perseverance leads to greatness.

Every young fan watching from the stands can learn something from these heroes—how to stay humble in victory, brave in defeat, and proud of who they are. Each swing, each catch, each smile carries a message of hope.

The legends of the Toronto Blue Jays remind every reader that dreams can come true with heart, hard work, and faith. Their spirit continues to soar across every stadium, inspiring young fans to chase their own baseball dreams.

CHAPTER 4: WORLD SERIES WONDERS

Every great team dreams of standing at the top, holding the championship trophy high for the world to see. For the Toronto Blue Jays, that dream came true—not once, but twice. Their World Series victories became moments of magic that united an entire nation in joy. These triumphs showed that with courage, teamwork, and faith, even the boldest dreams can soar higher than anyone imagined.

In the early 1990s, the Blue Jays had grown from hopeful newcomers into serious contenders. Each player carried the weight of a country's expectations, but also the support of millions of fans cheering them on. The city of Toronto buzzed with excitement, as if every heart beat in rhythm with the crack of the bat.

The road to glory wasn't easy. The team faced fierce opponents and challenging games, but their spirit never faded. They believed in one another and played with pride, heart, and determination. Every inning, every pitch, every hit brought them closer to greatness.

When victory finally arrived, fireworks lit up the night sky, and cheers echoed across Canada. The Blue Jays had done what no other team outside the United States had ever done—they became **World Champions**. That triumph lifted not only the players but the entire country into history.

Their second title came the following year, proving that their first win was no accident. Back-to-back championships turned the Blue Jays into legends, admired by fans young and old. Those seasons were filled with unforgettable plays, brave performances, and shining teamwork.

The World Series years remain a treasure in Blue Jays history—a reminder that success isn't just about talent, but about unity, effort, and an unbreakable belief in something greater than yourself.

4.1 The Road to 1992 Glory

The 1992 season was a story of determination. The Blue Jays entered the year focused and ready to prove they could be the best. Every practice, every game, and every challenge pushed them closer to their ultimate goal—a championship title.

Their lineup was full of talent. Players like **Roberto Alomar**, **Joe Carter**, **John Olerud**, and **Devon White** led the team with skill and confidence. Under the steady leadership of manager **Cito Gaston**, they learned that teamwork meant more than individual success. Together, they built something unstoppable.

The journey through the playoffs tested their strength. They faced tough teams and nail-biting moments, but the Blue Jays' courage never wavered. Each victory brought fans to their feet, waving flags and singing proudly for Canada.

When they reached the World Series against the **Atlanta Braves**, the stage was set for history. The games were intense, filled with drama and excitement. Every pitch felt like it carried the weight of the nation.

Then came the moment that changed everything—Toronto's triumph in Game 6. As the final out was recorded, the stadium erupted with cheers, tears, and pure happiness. The Blue Jays had done it—they were **World Champions for the first time ever**.

The 1992 victory wasn't just about winning a title—it was about making history. It showed that Canadian baseball could compete with the best and win with grace, heart, and pride.

4.2 The 1993 Home Run That Changed Everything

In 1993, the Blue Jays were ready to defend their crown. The season was thrilling from start to finish, filled with powerful plays, clutch moments, and the roar of loyal fans. The team was determined to prove their greatness once again—and they did, in unforgettable fashion.

The World Series that year matched Toronto against the **Philadelphia Phillies**. It was a battle of energy, strategy, and endurance. Both teams played with fire, refusing to give up an inch. The games were close, the crowds electric, and the excitement beyond imagination.

Then came the night that would live forever in baseball history—**October 23, 1993**. The Blue Jays were leading the series 3–2 and needed one more win to become back-to-back champions. The tension in the stadium was unbelievable.

In the ninth inning, with two runners on base, **Joe Carter** stepped up to bat. The count was tight, the pressure was heavy, and every fan held their breath. Then—*crack!*—the bat met the ball with perfect force. It soared high into the air, over the left-field wall, and into legend.

As Carter jumped for joy around the bases, the crowd erupted in celebration. The Blue Jays had just won their second consecutive **World Series Championship**—on a walk-off home run! The moment became one of the most iconic in all of baseball.

That swing wasn't just a victory for the team—it was a gift to every fan who believed. It reminded the world that courage and joy could create miracles in a single moment.

4.3 The City's Celebration of Victory

Toronto had never seen a celebration like the one that followed the Blue Jays' championships. The entire city came alive with happiness. Streets filled with fans waving flags, honking car horns, and singing songs of pride. For days, laughter and cheers echoed through every corner of the city.

People from every background joined the festivities. It didn't matter where they came from—everyone was united by one thing: love for their team. The victories brought together families, neighbors, and strangers, proving that sports can build bridges that nothing else can.

Downtown Toronto transformed into a sea of blue and white. Parades rolled through the streets, carrying players who waved and smiled at cheering crowds. Children held homemade signs, shouting the names of their heroes with excitement.

The celebrations stretched far beyond the city. Across Canada, people gathered in parks, schools, and community centers to share in the joy. Even fans who had never watched baseball before found themselves cheering, proud of what the Blue Jays had achieved.

Players and coaches thanked the fans for their love and faith. They knew the victories were shared—not just by those on the field, but by everyone who believed along the way.

The city's celebrations became a beautiful symbol of unity and happiness—a reminder that when people dream together, amazing things happen.

4.4 Lessons from Championship Moments

Every championship tells a story, and the Blue Jays' victories teach lessons that reach far beyond baseball. They show that success begins with teamwork, grows through effort, and blossoms through belief.

The players learned that winning isn't just about skill—it's about trust. Every throw, swing, and catch depended on working together. They supported one another through hard times and celebrated every triumph as a family. That unity was their greatest strength.

The coaches taught that discipline and patience build champions. They reminded players to stay humble in success and to learn from every mistake. True greatness, they said, comes from heart, not ego.

Fans learned something too. They discovered that faith and loyalty can lift a team higher than anyone imagined. Even during tough seasons, belief can spark miracles. Their cheers became part of the Blue Jays' victories, echoing across the country.

For young readers, the Blue Jays' story is a message of hope. It shows that dreams, when fueled by dedication, can truly come true. Every child who dares to dream big has the power to achieve something wonderful.

The World Series years live on as a shining example of what happens when courage meets teamwork. The Toronto Blue Jays didn't just win—they inspired generations to believe that every heart has the power to fly.

CHAPTER 5: TEAMWORK MAKES CHAMPIONS

Every baseball game is more than bats and balls—it's about trust, friendship, and unity. The Toronto Blue Jays learned early that no single player can win alone. It takes a whole team, working together, believing in each other, and giving their best to reach greatness. Teamwork is what turns effort into magic and dreams into victories.

From the dugout to the diamond, every voice matters. Players cheer for one another, coaches give guidance, and fans shout encouragement from the stands. Everyone has a role to play, and together, they create something powerful—something that can't be broken by setbacks or losses.

The Blue Jays built their success on this foundation of togetherness. Each player knew that their performance helped lift the entire team. When one person stumbled, another stepped up. When someone succeeded, everyone celebrated. That spirit of unity made every moment count.

Teamwork also means trust. On the field, every throw, catch, and swing depends on communication and confidence. The players rely on one another, knowing that their teammates have their backs. That connection transforms simple plays into unforgettable moments.

Young readers can learn from this too. Teamwork isn't just for sports—it's for school, friendship, and life. Helping others, sharing ideas, and believing in your group brings out the best in everyone.

The Blue Jays' legacy reminds us that true champions aren't made by one person's talent, but by many hearts beating together with a single purpose—to achieve something amazing as one.

5.1 The Power of Friendship on the Field

Friendship is the secret ingredient that keeps a team strong. On the field, friendships turn into fuel—lifting spirits, inspiring courage, and making every challenge feel possible. The Blue Jays showed that when players care about one another, the game becomes more than competition—it becomes joy.

Teammates share laughter in the locker room, jokes in the dugout, and high-fives after big plays. These small moments create trust that carries through tough times. When things get difficult, friends remind each other to stay positive and keep going.

Some players formed lifelong bonds while playing for the Blue Jays. They celebrated birthdays, shared meals, and supported each other through wins and losses. Those friendships didn't end when the games did—they continued off the field, built on respect and kindness.

Friendship also helps teams communicate better. When players trust each other, they can react faster and play smarter. One quick glance or nod can mean the difference between a great catch and a missed chance.

For young readers, this shows how important it is to be kind, loyal, and supportive. Friendship builds strength that no one can take away. Together, friends can face any challenge with smiles and confidence.

The friendships within the Blue Jays family remind us all that baseball isn't just about scoring runs—it's about sharing moments that make life brighter and hearts stronger.

5.2 Practice, Patience, and Perseverance

Every swing that hits a home run, every perfect throw, and every amazing catch begins with hours of practice. The Toronto Blue Jays didn't become champions overnight—they worked, trained, and believed, even when things were hard. Practice turned effort into excellence.

Players spent endless mornings running drills, sharpening their skills, and improving their focus. They practiced fielding grounders, hitting pitches, and studying strategies. Each repetition made them better, faster, and more confident. They knew that preparation was the key to victory.

Patience played an equal role. Baseball is a game of timing—waiting for the right pitch, choosing the right swing, trusting the right moment. The Blue Jays learned that rushing leads to mistakes, but patience brings success. They waited, watched, and trusted the process.

Perseverance meant never giving up, even when the score looked tough or the season seemed long. Every loss was a lesson, every setback a chance to grow. The team's never-quit attitude inspired fans to keep believing, no matter the challenge.

For kids, the Blue Jays' hard work is a powerful lesson: success takes time. Whether you're learning to read, draw, or play a sport, patience and practice will help you improve. Keep trying—you'll be amazed by what you can achieve.

The combination of practice, patience, and perseverance built champions. It's what made the Blue Jays more than just a team—it made them a symbol of hard work and heart.

5.3 Supporting Each Other Through Wins and Losses

Every season brings both joy and challenge. The Blue Jays learned to lift each other higher after wins and stand together during tough times. Their unity turned struggles into strength and triumphs into unforgettable celebrations.

When the team won, they celebrated as one. No victory belonged to a single player—it belonged to everyone who worked, trained, and believed together. The joy of a win was sweeter because it was shared. Smiles, laughter, and cheers filled the clubhouse after every success.

But the real test of character came during losses. When games didn't go as planned, the team didn't point fingers or give up. They encouraged each other, saying, "We'll get them next time." Coaches reminded players that mistakes were steps toward progress, not reasons to stop trying.

The Blue Jays showed that true teammates never leave anyone behind. They stood shoulder to shoulder, win or lose, knowing that unity mattered more than any score. That faith kept their spirit alive through long seasons and tough challenges.

For young readers, this teaches that life has ups and downs—but what matters most is how you handle them. Supporting friends through both success and struggle makes bonds unbreakable.

In the heart of every Blue Jays game lies a powerful truth: togetherness makes every moment brighter, no matter the outcome.

5.4 What It Means to Be a True Teammate

Being a true teammate goes beyond wearing the same jersey—it means caring, listening, and giving your best for others. The Toronto Blue Jays have always shown what real teamwork looks like through respect, effort, and heart.

A true teammate encourages others, celebrates their success, and helps them get better. When one player shines, everyone shines. The best teammates understand that every role matters, from star hitters to quiet helpers in the dugout.

The Blue Jays' players often talked about trust and attitude. They knew that winning starts with belief in one another. A good teammate lifts spirits, shares advice, and sets an example through hard work. They play for the name on the front of the jersey, not just the one on the back.

True teammates listen, communicate, and stay positive even when things get tough. They bring energy to practice, kindness to friendships, and strength to challenges. Their goal is not only to play well but to help others do their best too.

For young readers, being a great teammate means showing respect in every situation—on the playground, in the classroom, or at home. It means being there for others, even when things aren't easy.

The Blue Jays remind us that the greatest victories are won by teams filled with trust, love, and unity. Being a true teammate means shining together, dreaming together, and never forgetting that success is sweetest when it's shared.

CHAPTER 6: THE FANS WHO FLY HIGH

Every cheer, clap, and smile from the stands gives life to the game. The Toronto Blue Jays' fans are more than spectators—they are part of the heartbeat that keeps the team soaring. Their voices echo through every inning, turning the stadium into a sea of energy and pride. Without them, baseball would never feel as alive, as exciting, or as full of love.

From the very beginning, fans believed in the Blue Jays. They came to games through sunshine and rain, shouting encouragement with pure joy. Some waved flags, others wore painted faces, but all shared one goal: to lift their team higher. Every shout, song, and high-five became part of the Blue Jays' story.

Generations of families fill the Rogers Centre each season. Grandparents share stories of the early days, parents teach their kids how to cheer, and young fans dream of wearing the team's jersey someday. These connections make baseball more than a sport—it becomes a tradition passed down with pride.

When the team travels, fans follow. They fill other stadiums with blue and white, bringing the spirit of Toronto wherever they go. Their energy reminds players that no matter how far they travel, home is always cheering for them.

The Blue Jays' fans represent the power of loyalty. Win or lose, they stand by their team, proving that faith never fades. Their dedication shows the world that love for the game lives not only on the field but in every heart that beats for baseball.

Through every chant and clap, the Blue Jays' fans show what it truly means to belong. They don't just watch—they believe, they celebrate, and they fly high right alongside their team.

6.1 Young Supporters Around the World

Young fans are the heart of the Blue Jays' future. Across Canada and beyond, children wear caps, wave banners, and dream of hitting home runs. Their laughter fills the stands, their cheers light up the stadium, and their hope reminds everyone why the game is special.

Kids write letters to their favorite players, draw pictures of the Blue Jays logo, and practice their swings in backyards and schoolyards. Every little dreamer who picks up a bat adds another spark to the team's bright future.

The Blue Jays inspire young fans not only in Toronto but across the world. From small towns in Canada to cities overseas, children learn about teamwork, courage, and joy through baseball. They see how determination can turn ordinary moments into something unforgettable.

Players understand how important these young fans are. They wave at them during games, sign autographs, and visit schools to share their stories. Every smile from a player can create a memory that lasts a lifetime.

Many young fans join baseball programs that carry the Blue Jays' name, learning how to play with honesty, respect, and teamwork. Through these programs, kids discover that baseball isn't just about winning—it's about fun, friendship, and growth.

The next generation of Blue Jays supporters carries the same spirit of excitement and belief. With every cheer and dream, they help the team fly even higher into the future.

6.2 Game Day Traditions and Cheers

Game day in Toronto is always an adventure. From the moment the sun rises, the city buzzes with excitement. Families dress in blue, fans gather at restaurants, and children hold signs ready to show their love for the team. The Rogers Centre becomes a place where magic lives, and every heart beats to the rhythm of baseball.

As crowds fill the stadium, music plays, laughter spreads, and the smell of popcorn and hotdogs fills the air. Vendors call out with friendly voices, souvenirs sparkle under the lights, and fans settle into their seats, ready for the first pitch.

When the Blue Jays take the field, cheers roar like thunder. The famous chant—*"Let's go, Blue Jays!"*—rolls through the stadium, uniting thousands of voices. Each clap and shout gives the players extra strength, turning the field into a stage of inspiration.

During breaks, kids wave foam fingers, mascots dance, and families share high-fives. Even when the game gets tense, the crowd stays hopeful, singing songs that lift everyone's spirits. The togetherness of the fans makes every inning feel like a celebration.

At the end of the game, win or lose, fans stay to applaud the players. They know effort deserves respect, and their loyalty never wavers. The cheers that echo through the stadium remind the players that they are loved and supported.

Game day traditions are more than habits—they are joyful memories that connect people, build friendships, and remind everyone that baseball is about unity, fun, and pride.

6.3 Meeting Your Baseball Heroes

For many young fans, meeting a Blue Jays player is a dream come true. Whether it's a quick autograph, a photo, or a friendly wave, those moments can change a child's world. The players become more than athletes—they become heroes who inspire hope and happiness.

Before and after games, players often take time to greet fans. They smile, sign baseballs, and thank the crowd for their support. For kids, that handshake or signature becomes a treasure, a reminder that dreams are real and kindness matters.

The Blue Jays organize special events where children can meet players, ask questions, and learn about the game. These experiences encourage young people to stay active, work hard, and never give up on their goals. The players remind them that everyone starts somewhere—often with the same love for the game they now share.

Many heroes also visit hospitals, schools, and community centers to spread joy. Their words encourage kids to believe in themselves and to follow their passions with courage. They show that being a hero means helping others, both on and off the field.

For young fans, meeting a Blue Jays star can light a spark that lasts a lifetime. It's proof that kindness and effort can build connections between people from all walks of life.

The Blue Jays' heroes remind every fan—young or old—that dreams grow stronger when shared, and that every handshake holds the power to inspire greatness.

6.4 Sharing the Joy with Family and Friends

Baseball is more fun when it's shared. Families and friends come together to watch the Blue Jays, creating memories filled with laughter, excitement, and love. Each game becomes a special moment—a chance to connect, relax, and celebrate together.

Parents bring children to their first games, explaining the rules and cheering side by side. Grandparents tell stories of the old days, remembering famous players and historic wins. These moments build traditions that last through generations.

Friends meet up at the stadium or gather around televisions at home, wearing their favorite jerseys and sharing snacks. Whether in the stands or at a living room table, the joy is the same—the joy of being together, united by the team they love.

When the Blue Jays win, hugs, high-fives, and happy shouts fill the air. When they lose, fans comfort each other, saying, "Next time!" The bond between family, friends, and the team grows stronger with every season.

For young readers, these moments show how sports connect hearts. It's not only about scores or trophies—it's about togetherness, laughter, and friendship.

Sharing the joy of the Blue Jays reminds everyone that love for the game is meant to be shared. It brings people closer, fills hearts with warmth, and proves that baseball, at its best, is a celebration of family, unity, and dreams.

CHAPTER 7: THE FUTURE OF THE BLUE JAYS

Every new season brings fresh hopey, shining talent, and endless dreams. The Toronto Blue Jays continue to grow, blending experience with youthful energy. Their future sparkles with promise, as new players rise and fans cheer louder than ever. The story of the Blue Jays is still being written—one pitch, one hit, one victory at a time.

In the locker room, young players train beside seasoned veterans, learning lessons of courage, focus, and teamwork. The future is shaped by their shared determination to carry forward the team's proud legacy. They dream not only of winning but of inspiring the next generation of fans.

Technology, training, and teamwork combine to help these athletes reach new heights. Coaches use data to sharpen skills, players study every move, and together they build strategies that make the Blue Jays stronger each season.

As time moves on, the spirit of the Blue Jays remains the same—bravery, unity, and passion for the game. The future belongs to those who believe that greatness comes from hard work and heart.

Young fans watching from the stands or at home may one day wear the same uniform, swinging bats under the same sky. Every cheer they give today fuels tomorrow's champions.

The future of the Blue Jays is bright because it belongs to dreamers—those who never stop believing that anything is possible when you play with heart and fly with hope.

7.1 Rising Stars with Big Dreams

Every great team begins with a dream, and every player starts as a dreamer. The Toronto Blue Jays' future shines with rising stars who bring excitement, energy, and hope to the field. Their journeys inspire fans everywhere to reach higher, work harder, and chase their passions.

These young players train for hours each day, practicing swings, studying plays, and strengthening their minds. They know that becoming a Blue Jay means more than talent—it means commitment, teamwork, and character.

The team's scouts travel across countries to find these hidden talents—kids who play with love, dedication, and raw potential. Some come from small towns, others from big cities, but they all share one goal: to play for the Blue Jays and make their families proud.

When these players step onto the field for the first time, their hearts race with excitement. They wear the Blue Jays logo with honor, knowing they are part of something bigger than themselves—a family built on decades of hard work and hope.

Fans cheer as these new stars learn, grow, and shine. Some will become legends, others will inspire through effort and perseverance. Together, they represent the future of baseball in Toronto.

For young readers, their stories are proof that dreams come true with patience and purpose. Every swing, every throw, every heartbeat brings them closer to the moment when they, too, can soar like Blue Jays.

7.2 New Seasons, New Stories

Every spring, when the baseball season begins again, the world feels fresh and full of possibility. The Toronto Blue Jays step onto the diamond ready to write new chapters of courage and joy. Each season brings its own heroes, surprises, and unforgettable moments.

The players train all winter, waiting for that first pitch of the year. When the games begin, the stadium fills with excitement—the smell of fresh grass, the sound of bats cracking, and the roar of the crowd remind everyone that baseball is back.

New faces join the team each year, bringing new energy and new dreams. Fans learn their names, follow their progress, and celebrate every success. Each hit, catch, and home run adds another story to the team's growing history.

Some seasons bring championships, others bring lessons. Every win is celebrated, and every loss builds strength. What matters most is the journey—the teamwork, determination, and unity that keep the Blue Jays soaring.

Families, friends, and young fans all play a part in these stories. They fill the stands, wave banners, and share moments that will be remembered for years. Together, they help write the next chapter of the Blue Jays' incredible journey.

With every new season, hope begins again. The story never truly ends—it just keeps growing, one game, one dream, one heart at a time.

7.3 Training for Tomorrow's Wins

Behind every great play lies hours of unseen work. The Toronto Blue Jays know that the path to victory begins with training, focus, and discipline. Each player pushes their limits, determined to become better today than they were yesterday.

In the gym, they lift weights to build strength. On the field, they practice catching, throwing, and batting until every movement feels natural. Coaches guide them with patience, helping them refine skills and strengthen their confidence.

Training isn't just physical—it's mental, too. Players study strategies, learn from mistakes, and stay calm under pressure. They understand that baseball is a game of the mind as much as the body.

Nutrition, rest, and teamwork also play big roles. The Blue Jays' trainers teach players how to stay healthy, eat well, and recover properly. Taking care of the body helps keep the mind sharp and the spirit strong.

For young readers, the Blue Jays' hard work shows that success doesn't happen by luck—it comes from dedication. Practicing a skill every day, believing in progress, and learning from challenges can turn effort into excellence.

Every drop of sweat and every early morning practice builds the foundation for tomorrow's wins. The Blue Jays' training reminds us all that greatness is earned, not given.

7.4 Believing in the Next Generation

The future of the Toronto Blue Jays doesn't belong to just the players on the field—it belongs to the young fans who dream of wearing the team's colors one day. Every child cheering in the stands represents a spark of hope for the next generation of champions.

Players often say they play not only for themselves but for those who will come after them. They know that every hit, every game, every handshake inspires someone watching. Their effort becomes an invitation for others to believe in themselves.

The Blue Jays' youth programs and baseball camps help kids learn the game, build confidence, and discover the joy of teamwork. Coaches encourage them to dream boldly and to play with heart. Those small beginnings could one day lead to something extraordinary.

Parents, teachers, and mentors also play vital roles in nurturing those dreams. Their encouragement helps young people see that anything is possible with practice, patience, and positivity.

For every child who holds a bat, wears a cap, or imagines stepping onto the field, the dream of becoming a Blue Jay lives strong. The team's legacy continues through them—through every smile, every goal, every moment of belief.

Believing in the next generation means trusting that tomorrow's heroes are already here—ready to rise, ready to learn, and ready to keep the Blue Jays' spirit soaring into the sky of endless dreams.

CHAPTER 8: DREAM BIG, PLAY BOLD

Dreams begin with imagination and grow through courage. The Toronto Blue Jays have always shown that big dreams can lead to incredible victories. Their journey reminds fans everywhere that when you play with heart, believe in yourself, and never give up, anything is possible.

The Blue Jays' story is built on bravery. From their first game to their greatest wins, they've faced challenges with confidence and hope. They dared to dream beyond limits, showing the world that a small beginning can grow into a powerful legacy.

Playing bold means taking risks, trusting your instincts, and standing tall even when things seem difficult. The Blue Jays played boldly through tough seasons, always believing that better days were coming. Their courage turned struggles into strength and effort into triumph.

Every player, coach, and fan has been part of this bold spirit. Whether it's cheering from the stands or giving everything on the field, each person contributes to the team's dream of greatness. Together, they remind us that dreams grow stronger when shared.

For young readers, this is a lesson in courage. Dreaming big means imagining more for yourself—bigger goals, brighter futures, and endless possibilities. Playing bold means having the confidence to chase those dreams fearlessly.

The Blue Jays continue to prove that dreaming big and playing bold isn't just about baseball—it's about life. It's about believing that with effort, kindness, and teamwork, you can soar higher than you ever imagined.

8.1 Lessons from the Diamond

The baseball field, known as the diamond, is more than just grass and dirt—it's a classroom of life. Every inning, every pitch, and every play teaches lessons that go far beyond the game. The Toronto Blue Jays have learned and shared these lessons with millions of fans across generations.

The first lesson is **patience**. Baseball moves at its own rhythm. Waiting for the right pitch teaches focus and calmness. The Blue Jays learned that good things happen when you trust the moment and stay ready.

The second lesson is **teamwork**. No one can win alone. Each position matters, and every player must do their part. The Blue Jays' greatest victories came when they worked together, sharing effort and belief.

The third lesson is **resilience**. Sometimes the game doesn't go your way, but that's when strength grows. The Blue Jays learned to rise after every fall, to fight for every run, and to keep smiling no matter the score.

The fourth lesson is **joy**. Baseball is fun! The cheers, laughter, and friendships make every day at the diamond special. The Blue Jays never forgot to enjoy the game they love, even during challenges.

For every child watching, the diamond holds lessons for life—patience, teamwork, resilience, and joy. Those lessons, carried off the field, help build character, courage, and confidence for every dream ahead.

8.2 The Spirit of Never Giving Up

Great teams are built not just on skill but on spirit—the determination to never stop trying. The Toronto Blue Jays have faced hard seasons, close losses, and long roads to victory, yet they never gave up. That spirit has become their symbol, inspiring fans everywhere to keep going.

When games were tough and the score seemed impossible, the team kept playing with heart. They reminded everyone that the best moments often come after the hardest fights. Each comeback story, each thrilling win, showed the power of persistence.

Players trained harder, encouraged one another, and trusted that effort would lead to success. They understood that failure wasn't the end—it was just another step toward improvement. Every challenge was a chance to grow stronger.

Fans followed that same example. They believed through tough seasons, filling the stands with unwavering faith. Together, players and fans built a community that values hope over fear, action over doubt, and courage over quitting.

For young readers, this message shines bright: never giving up turns small dreams into big realities. Even when things seem hard, keep believing, keep trying, and keep smiling.

The Blue Jays' journey proves that strength comes not from winning easily, but from standing tall when the odds are against you—and flying higher every time you rise again.

8.3 Keeping the Dream Alive Beyond the Field

The Blue Jays' dream doesn't end when the game does. It continues in homes, schools, and playgrounds where young fans imagine themselves hitting home runs or making amazing catches. The spirit of the team reaches far beyond the diamond—it lives in hearts everywhere.

Players know that what they do inspires others. Their dedication, kindness, and teamwork encourage fans to chase their own dreams, whether in sports, school, or life. Each home run becomes a message: "You can do it too."

The Blue Jays also give back to communities. They visit hospitals, support youth programs, and help children discover the joy of playing baseball. Their kindness shows that success isn't just about trophies—it's about sharing hope and helping others.

Keeping the dream alive means holding onto the values that make the Blue Jays special—courage, unity, and joy. It means remembering that every dreamer matters and every effort counts.

Parents, teachers, and fans help carry this dream forward by encouraging kids to stay active, positive, and curious. Together, they ensure that the Blue Jays' legacy continues for generations.

The dream lives on every time a child swings a bat, cheers at a game, or believes in something bigger than themselves. That is how the Blue Jays' spirit keeps flying—bold, bright, and forever alive.

8.4 Every Fan's Journey Begins with a Cheer

Every fan's story starts with one moment—one cheer, one smile, one spark of excitement. For many, that moment begins when they first watch the Toronto Blue Jays take the field. From that day forward, their hearts belong to the team that plays with passion and pride.

The journey of a fan is filled with emotions—joy when the team wins, hope when they lose, and excitement for every new season. Each cheer, no matter how small, adds to the song of support that fills the stadium.

Being a fan also means being part of a family. Blue Jays fans share laughter, memories, and friendships that last a lifetime. Whether they watch from the stands, from home, or from miles away, their hearts beat together for the team they love.

Every young fan who picks up a glove or waves a flag is part of that journey. Their cheers encourage the players, and their dreams strengthen the Blue Jays' legacy. Each fan helps the team soar higher with every clap and shout.

The beauty of being a Blue Jays fan is that the journey never truly ends. Every game, every season, every new generation adds to the story. The connection between team and fan is forever.

So, to every young reader with a dream—remember this: your cheer is powerful. It carries hope, joy, and love. When you dream big and play bold, you join the Blue Jays' family of believers, flying high together under the bright sky of baseball dreams.

25 Fun Facts About the Toronto

Blue Jays 🐦 ⬤

1. The Toronto Blue Jays are **Canada's only Major League Baseball team**, representing an entire country instead of just one city.

2. The team was founded in **1977**, making them one of the younger MLB franchises.

3. The Blue Jays' name was chosen from over **30,000 fan suggestions** during a nationwide naming contest!

4. The **blue jay bird** was picked as the mascot because it's bold, bright, and full of energy—just like the team.

5. The Blue Jays won **back-to-back World Series titles** in 1992 and 1993—something very few teams have ever done.

6. In **1992**, they became the **first Canadian team to win the World Series**, making baseball history.

7. The famous **Joe Carter home run** in 1993 sealed their second championship—it's one of the

most legendary moments in baseball!

8. The team plays its home games at the **Rogers Centre**, which has a **retractable roof**—perfect for Canada's changing weather.

9. The Rogers Centre roof can open or close in just **20 minutes**, transforming the stadium from indoor to outdoor.

10. The Blue Jays' mascot is named **Ace**, a fun-loving blue bird who dances, jokes, and entertains fans at every game.

11. The team's colors—**royal blue, white, and red**—represent Canada's national pride and strength.

12. Before the Rogers Centre opened in 1989, the Blue Jays played at **Exhibition Stadium**, which was often windy and cold!

13. The Blue Jays' first game ever took place on **April 7, 1977**, and it actually **snowed** during the game!

14. Their first win came that same day, beating the **Chicago White Sox** 9–5, despite the snowstorm.

15. The Blue Jays have had some of baseball's biggest stars, including **Roberto Alomar, Joe Carter, Roy Halladay, and Vladimir Guerrero Jr.**

16. In 2015, **José Bautista's famous "bat flip"** became one of the most unforgettable moments in MLB history.

17. The Blue Jays' fans are known for their loyalty—they fill the stadium even during rebuilding seasons.

18. The team's minor league players develop their skills at the **Dunedin Complex** in Florida, where

spring training is held.

19. The Rogers Centre is one of the few stadiums where you can **watch a game from a hotel room** overlooking the field!

20. The Blue Jays' fan base stretches across **every Canadian province**, uniting the whole country under one team.

21. The team's logo has changed a few times, but it always includes the **blue jay bird** and a **red maple leaf** for Canada.

22. The Blue Jays' 1992 and 1993 championship rings feature **diamonds shaped like baseball diamonds**, symbolizing their triumph.

23. Their farm system helps young players grow—many stars, like **Bo Bichette and Vladimir Guerrero Jr.**, came from within their

own ranks.

24. The Blue Jays' games are broadcast in both **English and French**, making them truly bilingual ambassadors of baseball.

25. Every time the Blue Jays take the field, their motto shines bright: **"Let's Go, Blue Jays!"**—a cheer that brings smiles, pride, and hope to fans of all ages.

CONCLUSION

Flying High with Dreams and Heart

The Toronto Blue Jays' story is one of courage, teamwork, and belief. From their very first game in 1977 to the thrilling championships and unforgettable moments that followed, they've shown that big dreams can come true when you play with heart and never give up. Each swing, catch, and cheer has helped build a legacy filled with pride and hope.

Through every challenge, the Blue Jays stayed united. They learned that success isn't just about winning games—it's about growing stronger together, believing in yourself, and lifting others along the way. Their journey reminds fans that determination and kindness can turn even the smallest dream into something extraordinary.

For young readers, the Blue Jays are proof that every dream begins with one step. Whether you want to play baseball, write stories, sing, or explore the world, you can achieve it if you work hard, stay positive, and keep believing. Just like the Blue Jays, you can rise higher than you ever thought possible.

The fans, players, and coaches share one heart, one vision, and one passion—the love of the game. Their connection stretches beyond the field, reaching into homes, schools, and hearts across Canada and beyond. Together, they show that greatness grows when people come together with joy and purpose.

The Blue Jays' legacy continues with every new season, every new fan, and every dreamer who picks up a glove or waves a flag. Their story will keep inspiring generations to come—to fly higher, play bolder, and dream without limits.

So, young dreamers, always remember this: like the Blue Jays, you were born to soar. Keep believing, keep smiling, and keep chasing your dreams—because the sky is yours, and your story is only just beginning.

Manufactured by Amazon.ca
Acheson, AB

31491881R00052